DeClutter Your Life In 29 Days

A Minimalist Approach To Clear Your Home, Mind And Schedule

Amy Pendergrass

DEDICATION

Thanks Mom, for teaching me that the greatest step towards a life of happiness and simplicity is learning to let go.

.

CONTENTS

INTRODUCTION

The world we live in today is becoming a landfill of distraction – fast-paced, loud, bright, and with high stress levels. Each day is filled to the brim with social media, entertainment, technology, and even marketing. These factors seek out our attention, time, and focus. Ultimately, the mind is diverted and distracted from the things that actually matter – relationships, health, and work. If you can adopt certain principles that enable you to live a less distracted life, the world would definitely be a better place. It would become a place that is less congested and less agitating to the soul while making living more worthwhile.

Distractions are very easy to notice. I'm sure you can easily admit that you spend too much time watching television, checking your social media accounts, or even playing games on your phone. After all, the world is starting to become a battlefield for attention every single day. Aside from the obvious kinds of distractions, there are subtle distractions that surround us every day. These subtle distractions don't blow a horn or blink with bright lights. In fact, these distractions are so subtle that they have become an integral part of our daily routine, such that we barely notice their existence. But the sad truth is that these distractions occupy a significant space in our minds and distract us from pursuits in life that matter more. These distractions rob us of the chance of living our lives to the greatest potential.

Truly, far more damaging to our lives is the understated distractions that quietly surround us. These do not present themselves with beeping sounds or blinking lights. These distractions reside in our mind and cloud our focus in pursuing our goals.

CHAPTER I – EVER-PRESENT DISTRACTIONS

Distractions are usually present in everyone's lives. It is easy to identify such distractions, especially if any of them have already been part of your being. These distractions often lead to roadblocks in life and may clutter your mind, your life, and your overall perspective on living.

Tomorrow's Pre-Occupation
To make things clear, there is nothing wrong with looking forward to a bright and amazing tomorrow. The problem starts when we bear the present only for the sake of tomorrow. The biggest thief of life is the rat race of seeking comfort in the future. Why not appreciate what you have right now? Our mindset is suspended in a scenario that is about to happen; and if we cling to it, the sad truth reveals itself in front of us and shows that we are stuck in what we have now and feel dreadful about. By being so preoccupied with what the future could bring, we miss the potential and beauty of the present.

The Perfection Problem
It is human nature to pursue excellence and take pride in our achievements. Everything should be done with our best foot forward, and the next step should be the right step with as much intention as possible. However, achieving perfection and doing our absolute best are rarely the same. Whenever perfection becomes the goal, it becomes the enemy of progress. This scenario distracts us from moving on and

improving as individuals. We focus so much on getting to the destination that we no longer pay any heed to the journey. While we overthink the destination, we miss the beauty of the way that leads us to it.

The truth is that we feel strongly compelled to compare our lives with that of the people who surrounds us. Our belongings, how we look, our successes – it is an endless and tireless race that we all want to win. However, have you ever realized that every single time you focus on what others have, you energy and focus are diverted to the wrong person? In the end, nothing happens, and you are just drained of all the positivity and gratefulness for what you currently have. The powerful pull of comparison is a competition of life. Before, it was just survival of the fittest. Now, it is the war of success.

Regardless of how far our journey has been and how abundant our achievements and successes have been in the past, we cannot stop comparing ourselves with others. The reality of comparing yourself to others will always lead to regret about what you are not, when in fact there are so many things that you should be thankful for – things that have accomplished on your own on the journey toward success. Why not try to enjoy the progress you've had? It will surely make a huge difference in your outlook in life.

Minimalism of the mind – this is something that we secretly wish for. A mind less stressed is a mind that is not pre-occupied and a mind that perceives the better things in life. When we stop comparing, we focus our absolute best and energy into what we currently have and think of better ways to cultivate the successes, big or small, so that we can bring them to the next level.

The Pleasure that is Not
You may ask what is actually wrong with the pursuit of pleasure. Pleasure is good, until it goes over the top. Many individuals identify pleasure as one of the worst teachers in life. We tend to start with "just a little bit of pleasure," but

there is no such thing as "a little bit" when it comes to the pursuit of the pleasurable. We tend to engross ourselves because pleasure is something enjoyable, and we tend to go overboard. A sweet escape in the Caribbean, a holiday in Las Vegas, or carnival in Rio de Janeiro – these are just some of the typical pleasures outside of shopping, eating, and pampering. The most important lessons in life are rarely learned during times of pleasure.

The best lessons come from those painful memories of the past that tend to haunt us. Regrets, those small "what ifs" and "what could have beens" are just some of the lessons that are masked by pleasure. Pleasure is our vehicle to escape the harsh truths of reality. The sad truth is that it is not a permanent escape, and sometimes, we seek pleasure in all the wrong places; and these instances will just bear the fruit of more regrets in life.

The world we live in is a huge place and we as individuals have so much to give to it. However, there are those who would rather become the victim and, therefore, always miss their opportunity to give and to live completely. In addition, individuals who choose to embrace such unresponsiveness to the world around them will definitely miss out on harnessing their greatest potential. However, those who recognize their needs and try to seek and do something about it experience a sense of fulfillment and joy that can never be discovered elsewhere.

The Haunting Yesterday
Our lives are peppered with regret, even if we choose not to admit it. Those little regrets, what ifs, should haves, and could haves taint our emotions and haunt us as we deal with our daily lives. There are decisions, actions, and even motivations that we regret. However, it is very important to remember that no amount of regret can ever change what has happened in the past. Past is past, and we can only be hopeful about what tomorrow brings.

You should only consider regrets as imperfections along the way, not as a definition of who you are as an individual. By calling your mistakes as they are and recognizing them as stepping stones that have molded you into what you have become today, the haunting can soon stop. We should not allow regret to distract us from the opportunities that lie in front of us. Regret will only bring us hesitations, which often lead to more regrets in the future. To live is to experience regret — nobody escapes life unscathed. Remember that no amount of regret can ever modify the past no matter how much you think about it and reflect on it. Only individuals who have come to identify and acknowledge their failures are able to move beyond them. Call your mistakes what they are, embrace them, offer an apology when necessary, and then move on. Do not allow any remorse from the past to distract you from the opportunities of today.

Possessions that Pile Up

That ticket when you first traveled abroad, the first issue of your favorite magazine, a signed poster from your favorite football player, a random dry leaf you picked during one of your autumn trips – these things bear good memories, but they do pile up. There are a lot of things we own that will eventually require all our energy, attention, money, and, most importantly, time. As our possessions increase, our stress levels also increase.

Many people have always believed that having more is living better, which is wrong in more ways than one. Accumulated possessions yield stress, life issues, and even conflicts. This is something we know, yet we still go for the temporary satisfaction that the accumulation of possessions can bring. The things we own require our time, space, energy, money, and attention. We need to remember that having more is equal to becoming more distracted.

Individuals who chase their greatest dreams have the highest possibility of misplacing their potential and just giving in to the shiny offer and the highest bidder. Remember the phrase, "if your dreams don't scare you, they are not big enough"? There is a grain of truth in it, but you're just looking at the tip of the iceberg. We have been programmed to be social individuals who serve a particular purpose and chase a specific passion. Unfortunately, due to the world's ever-changing standards, we start becoming derailed from the path toward our goals and aspirations.

The objective of living and leaving a positive impact on society is slowly fading. The truth is, our contributions only focus on the financial side of things. When our self-imposed contribution to society is primarily motivated by selfish goals and desires, we turn into self-focused individuals. This desire and reality inhibits us from living our lives to the fullest.

Regardless of whether anybody actually notices what you have been doing all your life, the life you live is the life that no one can rob from you. Nothing will change if someone watches over your successes or failures. You are at the wheel. Those who live lives focused on the need to be acknowledged are usually the individuals who take shortcuts just to get there. Instead of doing this and being trapped in a vicious cycle, try to find significance in the eyes of those who know you best and know you deeply—because in the end, significance is all that matters anyway.

The reality of today is that our world is full of distractions – lots of them – in all shapes and sizes. And the most dangerous kinds are those we do not recognize at all.

CHAPTER II – THE BEAUTY IN SIMPLICITY

"It is desirable that a man live in all respects so simply and preparedly that if an enemy take the town... he can walk out the gate empty-handed and without anxiety."

-Henry David Thoreau

Simplicity is one of the most underrated principles today. Simplicity brings balance, freedom, and joy. Once we begin to live a quaint and simple life and experience these wonderful benefits, we start to ponder on next step: "I wonder where else in my life I can reduce distractions and how I can concentrate on the essential."

According to experts in living a minimalist life, there are 10 very important aspects that you should assess and validate so that you will able to enjoy living a joyful and balanced lifestyle. Minimalism is not just about reducing material things. It refers to a complete transformation from cluttered to being simple, inside and out.

Possessions
The more material possessions we have, the more complicated our lives get. These things can drain our finances, attention, effort, and time. Materialistic living robs

us from devoting our time, money, and effort to the people and things that truly matter. In a world smothered by technology, convenience, and lots of distractions wrapped in fancy packaging, it can be a tough battle to reduce our possessions or at least control our materialistic mentality. The temptation is too strong, as some may say; but if you will look at the grand scheme of things, possessions can actually possess you and your life.

If you can only divert your investment in possessions into something more essential, like your health and family, it can be one of the greatest decisions in life that you'll ever make.

Commitments

Most of us have schedules filled with commitments for the next several weeks, with some even having their calendars full for the upcoming months and years. Before we sleep, our minds are already cluttered with things we should do tomorrow, the next day, the next month, and even that event next year. These things inhibit us from having a good night's sleep because the list is so long that our minds work overtime and will never achieve that restful sleep our bodies so need. Like possessions, this can be tough to segment and simplify. But if you can free yourself from some of the commitments that do not jive with your values in life, or those that can simply be canceled out, your mind and body will thank you for it.

Goals in Life

Our so-called life goals are great, until the things we want to achieve in life heavily burden our minds. According to experts in minimalism, there is a thin line between preparing a list of attainable goals and messing them up because they are too numerous to achieve realistically. Less goals allow you to focus your attention on more important things. Reducing your goals also increases your success rate significantly. An old proverb says that if you chase two rabbits, you'll end up with none. This is also applicable to goals and aspirations in life. Get enough goals to keep you inspired, and just enough not to keep you distracted or exhausted. It is also a good idea to list your goals – it doesn't matter if they are long or short-term. Cross out those you've been able to accomplish, then replace them with another goal. Achieving these goals is like playing a game in which you unlock a specific "achievement" and then move forward once you have completed a task. It creates a simpler and more systematic approach to life.

Negativity

Negative thoughts are like rocks. They come in different shapes, sizes, and weights. These are totally useless emotions that give us a heavy heart. The rocks of jealousy, hate, resentment, and bitterness will never do us any good. These emotions clutter our minds and hearts, and they become daily emotional baggage we have to deal with over and over again. No one can tell you to unpack your emotional baggage, because this decision should come from you. It is okay to get hurt. The problem starts when we keep on hurting ourselves with the pain of what yesterday has been. You must learn to forgive yourself for the mistakes you've made in the past. Make amends with the past and try your very best to replace negative thoughts with something more fruitful and positive. You will be surprised how light each day will become if you dwell on the things that make you smile. You will be much happier when you know how to move on and close a chapter rather than keep on re-reading chapters of bad memories. Reminder, your mind and your happiness are your responsibility.

The Mountain of Debt

Debt can be your best friend or your worst enemy depending on how you treat it. If debt is preventing you from maximizing your financial control, reduce it. There is no other best day to start but today. The sooner you start controlling and reducing your debt, the sooner you'll break free and take control. By sacrificing some of the luxuries of today, you are saving a great deal of financial freedom tomorrow. Debt is something you can discuss with a financial advisor, who can guide you in terms of the things you need to prioritize when dealing with debt.

Word Count
Who would have thought that fewer words mean less emotional burden? By speaking fewer, yet more meaningful words, you maintain an honest and plain conversation. Avoid gossip wherever you go, whether in the neighborhood, the office, or somewhere else. If other people initiate the gossip, don't fight fire with fire. A minimized use of words defines a person's maturity and wisdom. When you control your tongue and speak only when necessary, people tend to believe that your words carry more weight. The old saying can't be more true: Less words, less mistakes.

Artificial Ingredients
By avoiding artificial ingredients like preservatives, refined grain, too much salt, and trans-fats, we improve our overall health and energy levels. This keeps our body simple and healthy. Simple means less illness to worry about in the future. There are so many ingredients available on the market nowadays that can add flavor to your food, but it cuts years off your lifespan. Also, try not to self-medicate whenever you have minor illnesses such as a cough and cold. Over the counter medications can provide relief, but these medications also come with adverse reactions. There are better home remedies that can work for you and save you, not just from the potentially harmful reactions, but from the dependency of taking medications for simple ailments as well.

Turn off the Technology
Right now, we are living in a modern age where technology gives us everything in an instant. This amazing convenience, whether in terms of connecting with people, having great entertainment choices, video games, and even ease of preparing food, is a great restructuring factor in life. However, because of convenience, we tend to absorb it as part of our routine, and we end up not functioning properly if it is not available. We wake up in the morning, and the first

thing our eyes gaze on is the screen of our mobile phones. We have so many connections and friends in social media, but I highly doubt that the situation is the same in real life. When you allow technology to become your norm, you will have a hard time dealing with life without it. You tend to chase the latest thing in technology and fail to focus your attention on those that matter. Gadgets wear out, your favorite TV series ends, but your life goes on. You will only realize the problem of dependency once life is all you have, which can either be a liberating experience or a meltdown waiting to happen.

Double-check Your Bridges
In connection to the previous factor, which is technology, now is the perfect time to double-check your bridges or connections. Relationships, no matter where in the world, are actually good. However, if they start to become a distraction, then you have a problem. Learning to burn bridges, especially the bridges that lead you into uncertainty or to unhealthy relationships, will benefit you in the long run. It is like clearing your garden of weeds and allowing the beautiful flowers to grow. Remember: focus on what is important, and not what is urgent. Due to the constant supply of distractions from other people, we actually feel needed, important, or even wanted. This leads to several things. On the social networking site Facebook, opinions vary from one person to another, and what you see online can be different from your opinions and values. In the end, you become distracted. Light your fire and start burning now.

Multi-Tasking Disaster
The art of multi-tasking looks good on paper. Imagine dealing with several things all at once. In reality, the art of multi-tasking is equivalent to messing around with several things at once. You lose focus, and there is a high tendency of not giving your very best because there are so many different things on your plate. Distributed effort leads to mediocre results. Single tasking is a rarity nowadays, but this is

something you should learn and learn to love. Once given a task, put your best foot forward. Once you are done, you are now ready to tackle the next one. You will be amazed at how productive and amazing your output will be compared to that in the days when you hoarded tasks and ended up not doing any of them in a manner that exceeded expectations.

CHAPTER III – WHERE TO START

The idea of living a simple, stress-free life with less things to worry about sounds very appealing to many. However, when they get to the point of actually determining where to start, uncertainty is their major roadblock, and they end up not doing it at all because of several factors. It can be fear, because people tend to be too scared to let go of relationships, things, and even goals. It could be an overwhelming feeling because it is like starting all over again. The concept of living with less possessions branches out into several advantages aside from less time needed to organize, less time required to clean, less maintenance, more energy, and more money to pursue personal goals and passions. You can be physically ready to restart your life for the better, but are you emotionally ready?

Where should I Begin?
This question can painfully resonate for individuals who have been hoarding all their lives – a memorable ticket, a favorite shirt, that trophy from the summer games, a random twig from a trip up north. Your journey toward decluttering should not be as painful as others tend to exaggerate. Actually, you can start according to your preferred pace. Some can do a 180-degree turn in a week, whereas others may need several weeks.

There are numerous ways to start decluttering, but you may want to have a look at the ways I will be citing here to make it less painful. This can get you working on your way to a simpler life. Leo Babauta, a well-known advocate of minimalism, has been helping many people live a decluttered life. These recommendations have been collected for your convenience to get you on the fast track to a more breathable and less cluttered life.

Breathing and How it Transforms Life

Breathe. This is one of the things we tend not to remember because we've been so busy attending to our responsibilities and distractions. Breathing has the power to transform your life, by releasing tension and focusing on what is important. Whenever you feel stressed out or if you feel overwhelmed, breathe. Breathing allows you to be calm. If you are worrying about the things that might happen or things that have already occurred, just breathe. This allows you to escape from the burden and focus on the present.

If you feel discouraged or seem lost, try to breathe. Breathing is not just an exchange of oxygen into our cells; it is like a refresher for our minds, a reassurance that everything will be fine. It will remind you of the happier moments, and it will replay the things you have been able to resolve. There is also one important thing that breathing brings to us: it reminds us that as long as we are still breathing, everything will be okay. Even in your worst days, you are still alive and can weather that day in the hopes of having a better one. Just do not forget to breathe, and don't forget the better side of things in life.

One Item a Day Policy

If a massive decluttering brigade sounds over the top for you, try the one item a day policy. There are several patterns available online and in books, but you can totally customize your own schedule. Bear in mind, however, that this approach should be one item a day for an entire year. By simply giving up a single item each day, you are on a journey of transforming your life into something messed up to one more simple and organized.

One Trash Bag – like a Big One
Try to find the biggest trash bag you can get, and do not stop adding items into the bag until you have completely filled it. This will allow you to contemplate things that have been hanging around for years, and you will realize that you don't actually need them.

The Closet Hanger Experiment by Oprah Winfrey
This is not an Oprah Winfrey original, but she was able to highlight this kind of wardrobe experiment. Do this by yourself by hanging all your clothes in reverse direction. Then, return the clothes in the correct direction after you wear them. After about six months, the reversal of clothing articles will provide you with a better view of what items you can discard easily. This can also be applied to other things that heavily clutter your living space, such as linens, toys, tools, and even crafts.

The Great List
The great list is like compartmentalizing your home and decluttering from the easiest to the hardest: this gets you going. According to experts, decluttering can be a very time-consuming task, with most time wasted in identifying the room in which you should start. You can start with what you think can be physically and emotionally easy for you. Stockrooms are usually considered as bad decluttering starters because this is the typical room where memorable items are placed. The organization of the easiest to hardest room to tackle is subjective, and the creation of a list depends on your schedule.

Twelve by Twelve by Twelve Challenge
This is a relatively easy approach and less stressful as well. The twelve by twelve by twelve challenge is a project wherein you determine the following every single set:

12 Things to Donate
12 Things to Throw Away
12 Things to Return

By segregating these things every so often, it becomes easier to let go of things because the two-thirds that you segregate will go somewhere equally purposeful. Donating things like an old favorite dress or a toy will go a long way, and it will be easier to let go knowing that someone will receive the possessions you have donated or returned. Individuals that are new to minimalism undergo a painful ordeal because they feel as if they are throwing away things that matter to them. This method decreases the emotional struggle brought on by the sentimental items that are being given away.

If you think you cannot actually throw away things, then you can either expand the items that will be donated or returned. You can also reconsider upcycling or repurposing items before giving them to others. This will definitely give rise to a win-win situation because you are able to unload a lot of the stuff you own, and you can give things you don't necessarily need to others who may need them.

A Different Perspective

By looking at your home in a different light, you allow a refreshing new perspective to take root. You can then apply this perspective as you change, discard, or donate some of the usual things that can be found in your space. Some of the resources available online offer creative ways to allow individuals to see their own homes and offices from a different perspective.

Take a picture of your home and its rooms and then have them printed. Make sure that you have the photos printed such that you are not just staring at your computer screen or camera phone. Then, brainstorm how you can reduce all the drab and clutter. Do this one room at a time.

Ask a neighbor to visit your place with a toddler or someone you are not completely close to. Observe where their eyes lead them, because usually when a room is overcrowded with clutter, chances are they will say it. Reorganization of your rooms will also allow natural light to come in, and it makes the room simpler and more lively.

Ignore Your Inbox
Do not make your e-mail inbox as your task compass for the day. This is one chronic problem encountered by employees every single day without them completely understanding the impact this has on their physical and emotional well-being. Individuals who focus on the inbox are prone to multi-task and are likely not doing well or not accomplishing anything at all. This is a common scenario. Because of the lack of productivity or quality that barely exceeds the required standard, stress and emotional burden build up.

Banish Procrastination
Don't be a pro in procrastination. We are all guilty of this, even if we do not completely admit it. Procrastination consumes a lot of essential time to get the job done. It is the kryptonite of individual's productivity, and it will lead you to nowhere but more backlogs. Think happy thoughts, and when I say happy thoughts, I mean those things that motivate you to work and keep you focused on what you are doing.

The Numbers Game
Like the twelve by twelve by twelve method, there are other approaches we can employ with the use of numbers. One classic example is Courtney Carver's Protect 333, which challenges individuals to only wear thirty-three articles of clothing for three months. This can be adjusted more or less, but the important lesson here is to challenge yourself to live with less than usual and learn from it. Eventually, you'll love living a life less cluttered.

Ask Yourself
Asking yourself some unique questions can ease up on

decluttering the most difficult things to remove. Unique questions such as "how much will this be if I'm buying this now?" and other creative techniques can help remove the long overdue clutter that has been sitting around your living space for quite some time.

The Four Boxes Technique

This is similar to the twelve by twelve challenge, only segregated into four boxes. The boxes are split into four categories:

A Box for Trash
A Box for Donation
A Box for Relocation
A Box for Keeps

This can work for some, although it can be a problem for individuals who are very sentimental because they might end up filling just one box – which is the box for keeps. There are projects that can take as little as an hour, whereas others may take weeks or months. As long as you keep on segregating and moving on, you're on the right track.

The Timer Technique

This is specifically meant for individuals who treasure too much and invest too much emotion on things that need to be disposed of or relocated. Each time you have an item that has become a decluttering roadblock, contemplate on it for just one full minute. Dwelling on it for a longer amount of time will only branch out emotions, and you would end up not discarding any more items. There are things that do need to go. You just have to prioritize what is more valuable to you as a person as compared to other things.

No matter what method you choose to start your decluttering, the most important thing here is to take the first step. Everything will follow once you start your journey. Imagine looking forward to the simple, refreshing, and free world that awaits you after you successfully unload some of the burdens you have in life, whether materialistically or emotionally. How you declutter your life will still depend on your conscious choice to do so.

CHAPTER IV – THE SIMPLE WAY OF LIFE

Most people consider minimalists as people who live with fewer things around them, and that's about it. What they do miss in living a simple life is that the freedom to enjoy life and immerse oneself in the experience of living simple is a completely new experience. People who live simple lives are healthier, more appreciative, and very optimistic. Whenever you put your focus on the good things in life while being under the influence of simple living, you are enjoying something that money can never afford.

There are several things that can be considered to unbusy yourself. Unbusying is the art of unloading physical and emotional burdens, and creating a steady and strong beam of attention toward the tasks that can be singlehandedly dealt with. You are in for a treat because when you focus instead of divide, your work performance improves, your life becomes more organized, and your days will be more fruitful. Below are some guides to help you on your way to becoming an unbusy person.

Consider this Helpful Guide to Becoming Unbusy:
In case you forget, remember that being busy is a matter of choice. This is something we decide for ourselves. We make ourselves busy. No one can force us into an environment that drowns us in busyness. The most important step to becoming

a less busy person is to realize that you can determine your own schedule. This applies both at home and at work. You don't wake up to a pre-determined and pre-planned routine automatically. What you do depends on you. You have a choice, to get busy or not at all.

However, an unbusy person and someone who is lazy are two very different individuals. An unbusy person is someone who is still productive, whereas a lazy person accomplishes nothing. An unbusy person feels lighter every time a task is done, whereas a lazy person piles up the work.

Kill the Idea of Busy = Productive
This is something that has been going on for decades. The term "busy" is always associated with success and wealth. That is not always the case. There is a big difference between working hard and working wise. Actually, if we will focus on the idea that being busy is the clear path to success, we are unfortunately going nowhere, especially if our efforts are directed toward the wrong objectives and motives. Just like other minimalists have exclaimed – it is mighty fine not to be busy.

Rest Days are there for a Reason
Rest days are there for a reason that almost all employees seem to forget. Nowadays, we fail miserably when it comes to recognizing and appreciating the value and importance of rest. Rest days enable us to physically and emotionally relax from the things that have been brought by day to day activities, particularly in the office. While others justify that they get enough sleep each day, rest days offer a different kind of reparation and de-stressing. The more you deprive your body of rest, the more susceptible you are to acquiring illnesses and premature wear and tear. Even mechanical objects need maintenance, and this shows that rest is all the more necessary for us humans. You must guard your rest days with all your might. These days, as well as vacation leave, should be sacred. There are lots of people nowadays who extend their work into their rest days, which totally

defeats their purpose. This does not signify dedication to work – you tend to forget that it is your right to have a restful rest day. Consider it as recuperation to be physically and mentally prepared for the next week's tasks.

Reconsider Your Priorities

The only constant thing in this world is change. Change is actually good, unless you don't befriend it at all. For individuals who are resistant to change, adapting to today's ever-changing tides may be such a difficult feat to accomplish. These tides can rattle life goals or even destroy their virtues. Take time to reconsider your priorities, if they still fits the bill. Reconsideration is very important because the reality is that there are priorities no longer worth pursuing. By checking on the self-imposed goals you want to achieve by a certain age or time, you can weed out stressors and allow better ideas and objectives to grow and flourish. Bear in mind that smaller and more attainable priorities are much, much better than massive ideas that never come to life.

A review about your own personal priorities should not be rushed. This is something you need to accomplish by taking a seat, breathing, and then listing down your objectives in life. This is about your future and how you will mold the aspects you have full control over. This is a part of your life that busyness keeps interfering with by clouding your thoughts and causing you to lose your way.

Fewer but Better Possessions

You have no idea how much energy it takes to process your surroundings whenever you have so many things around you. It is true that the more things you own, the more time it takes to attend to them. Things need to be maintained, cleaned, organized, and arranged. These actions require a lot of time, and by the time you know it, a day has already passed. Why not try to own fewer things? In doing so, you will gain more time for yourself. You can find more time to appreciate and enjoy the freedom of having less. Again, you don't have to live under a rock to live modestly. Fewer but better possessions are more worthwhile than many low-quality possessions. It pays to check labels and quality standards. A reasonably priced dress is better than multiple inexpensive clothes that wear out a lot faster. This saves you money, space, and time.

Allow More Time

You may think that you are receiving mixed signals because we've been discussing how to live a better life by saving time as one of the most important aspects. What I am trying to point out here is that you should allocate more time for the important things. I'm sure a lot of us skip lunch because we're such workaholics. For those who don't, they tend to do speed-eating sessions just to catch up with the time-in. These are some of the bad office habits that have become deeply ingrained in our routines, such that we already consider them normal.

Some of the most common illnesses that are work-related are stomach ulcers and hyperacidity due to missed meals. These illnesses may lead to more serious complications that could ultimately lead to hospitalizations. Plus, they could have been prevented in the first place if we didn't skip a meal or hurry it. By allowing more time to appreciate meals, you allow your body to function better. This applies to both breakfast and lunch, which are the more commonly missed meals by office workers. Allowing more time to eat also enriches relationships, appreciation of food, and less gastronomic strain. You know what is even better? Try preparing your own lunch. It makes each day more of a "personalized" experience from sun up to sun down.

Another better allotment of your precious time is for meditation or any hobby that lies in close relationship with nature. Consider having meditation or yoga sessions. These activities can act as an outlet for daily stress, frustrations, and tension. They promote discipline and serenity. You can also try to detach yourself every once in a while, and to learn more about yourself and become more acquainted with your own physical limits and mental potential. A staycation is great, although workaholics have a high tendency to break the rules of having a staycation by working instead. Allowing more time for yourself means that you would be following a personal discipline. Your body is your best asset. Use it, but don't abuse it.

The Autonomy of the word "No"

There is something about saying no that makes us reluctant to do it, and, instead, we tend to give in to the strong force of saying yes. Humans are emotional by nature, and we tend to be eager to please others. It is common for a lot of individuals to make quite an ordeal out of just saying this two-letter word. We must recognize the importance of saying no and realize that in life, there are situations in which we really have to say it. This allows you to focus on more important things and prevent yourself from suffering from the additional stress that will derail your thoughts. We are always afraid of the thought that saying "no" will cause us to hurt someone's feelings. There is a grain of truth in this, but you have to remember that sometimes, saying no is for your own good, especially in situations where you cannot commit your very best. Starting today, try to say "no." However, this response should not be abused. We should still be cautious in our decisions whether to decline and when to go on.

We now live in a very busy environment, but that should not define who we are. In a life that is fast-paced and busy to the greatest extent, it is ok to have a calm and unbusy life. A calm oasis in a scorching busy world, how refreshing is that? That oasis can be you.

CHAPTER V – DE-OWNING, DE-CLUTTERING, AND ORGANIZING: DEFINING DIFFERENT PATHS

The world in which we live is a sea of people drowning in ambitions and possessions, and it is such a difficult task for many to appreciate the best things in life. We tend to become emotional and sentimental, and we take in and accumulate lots of stuff from parties, sales, birthdays, and anything else you can think of. However, although we receive many opportunities to take in, we cannot seem to find the chance to discard any of these accumulated possessions.

De-owning and de-cluttering are two essential aspects of living simply. De-owning is more about reducing your material possessions, whereas de-cluttering is a complex combination of reducing your emotional, physical, and mental loads. You should master these paths because they have to work hand in hand for you to be able to reach the ultimate goals of minimalism.

De-owning, as we have previously discussed, can be done using different approaches depending on your emotional tolerance. We have the number and timer methods that can help you reduce the number of thing you own significantly in a tolerable rate. But if you are a brave soul, you can courageously skim through your things, segregate, and either dispose of or donate them.

On the other hand, if we are content with organizing our current possessions, below are some of the shortcomings that should be taken into consideration. You will notice that this is like a flat tire; you cannot go anywhere until you do something about it – which is to change it by changing your perspective in life.

Because things will only move around the house and will not go anywhere, do not expect that they will benefit anyone at all. The things that you own will only sit in the spaces of your house, on the shelves, in the attic, or in that large basement. De-owning can actually help your neighborhood or even close friends because you might have something they badly need.

Because there is no viable movement of your possessions, it will not do anything related to debt. Selling things you don't actually need but have been sitting for quite a long time can actually go a long way. Having your own garage sale or participating in community market activities can help you unload the things you don't use often and earn cash from them. The amount of money you can get from the things you decide to de-own will completely depend on you. This can range from small amounts of cash that can be used to start a savings account, to something significant enough to allow you to have financial stability for the rest of the year.

Organizing will not inhibit our desire to become attached
Because there is no direct loss in organizing our possessions that we simply place in closets, boxes, and bins, it does not affect our living parameters. Our minds just become set on the thought that we have never lost anything.

Organizing is basically a band-aid solution
This method does not allow us to assess our lives. Rearranging will not raise any questions because when we

close a lid or seal another box, the memories remain. This is just a band-aid solution waiting for a more concrete and logical action to have a life-changing experience. The scenario is very different once we start removing our possessions by either giving them away or selling them. This will definitely raise questions about memories, passion, personal values, and what really matters to us.

After discussing the aspects of the choice to merely organizing your possessions, we now move on to the aspects of de-owning and de-cluttering.

De-owning is the start of freedom

Freedom of space, time, effort, and more – these are just some of the advantages of de-owning. You may think that de-owning even the littlest of things will not mean a lot, but it can actually become a spark of emotional maturity in terms of living simply. De-owning will give you freedom from the time needed to tend to things that could've been disposed of sooner. Freedom is such an underrated word that is strongly celebrated by the discipline of having a minimalist life.

De-owning is a rejuvenation of life

Whenever you de-own material things, you rejuvenate your life by somehow reclaiming your focus and energy. You allow yourself to freshen up and regain your attention from the things that surround you, such that you can instead focus on yourself and your goals in life. De-owning some of your possessions is just the tip of the iceberg in terms of the changes and benefits you will reap. To see the greater perspective is to appreciate life by living less.

De-owning brings out the essence of being human

Charity and giving are some of the core values of de-owning. Even if you are selling stuff rather from donating or giving it away, you still give something that matters to you. De-owning promotes compassion, and it makes you realize that giving goes a long way. We've heard of stories in which de-owners gave away boxes of clothes than went from the

United States to less fortunate individuals in other countries. While those recipients cannot thank you personally, the idea of your possessions reaching others in need is already something heartwarming.

De-cluttering will burn bridges
Yes, it will. If this fact scares you, then you should go for it. We live in a world where we tend to please others even if they act as roadblocks for our lives. Then these bridges deserve to be burned more than ever. This is one of the most important aspects of living simply. There are heavy burdens that cannot be cleared by sending them away or putting them in a box, because they rest inside our hearts and minds. There will always come a time when you have to chop off some ties, burn some bridges, and unfriend some connections to be completely happy. You will never experience true happiness until you try.

De-cluttering is a seed that is there
We all have this tiny seed inside our hearts. This is not the de-cluttering seed, but the seed of happiness that has been waiting to sprout freely. You know what prevents it from growing? Our negative thoughts and burdens in life that include material things and emotional baggage. Let that seed grow, and you will finally experience the true meaning of living a happy life.

CHAPTER VI –BENEFITS OF MINIMALISM

Let's do a brief recap of our previous chapters. Always remember that minimalism is something considered as countercultural. We are aware that the commercials we see on TV highlight the idea of having lots of things as the definition of a happy and meaningful life. That is something that is totally the opposite of what it takes to live a purposeful life. A great life cannot be defined by tons of possessions, but of the significance of your contributions and your immersion in what life is all about. Here are some of the benefits of a minimalist life that you might tend to overlook. Keeping these in mind can release you from thoughts that are keeping you from letting go of some of your possessions.

Low Cost
Minimalism allows you to spend less on things that are unimportant. Splurges and compulsion are controlled. In the long run, spending less can be your golden ticket to financial freedom, which everyone dreams of having. Financial freedom is everyone's dream, yet not everyone is courageous enough to find ways to achieve it.

Low Stress
Of all the minimalist families we have reached, we have yet to see one that has been living a life as stressful as their previously cluttered one. The homes of minimalist

individuals are dramatically less stressful because there are a lot less things to think about. This allows relationships to flourish more, because the focus of attention now goes to the members of the family and not to the materialistic side of the home.

Low Maintenance

Families that live under the discipline of minimalism are in for a treat. Because of the reduction in material possessions, the requirement for maintenance is also significantly lower because there are fewer things to clean. A home that has less things will also have less accumulation of dust, and a home with a lot of open space allows for better air circulation and natural light.

More Freedom

Freedom cannot be stressed enough. Less things to think about leads to freedom of mind. Single tasking in the office gives freedom of time and increased productivity. Less debt earns your way into financial freedom.

Environment Friendly

Minimalism allows families to consume less household items, such as cleaning agents and other potentially-harmful chemicals. This means that a minimalist household promotes an environment-friendly lifestyle.

Plus for Productivity

Because our time and effort are focused on fewer but more important things, we allow ourselves to pursue our passions, which we seem to have been chasing for a long time but never seem to reach. This is because we don't have enough time due to the burdens of distraction and possessions. Instead of arranging and organizing innumerable possession, why not rekindle an old hobby or write an inspirational book?

A Discipline for the Next Generation

Minimalism can be something that the next generation will

thank you for. It is a kind of discipline that your children will appreciate, as it provides lessons and experiences that no amount of technology or any type of media can offer. These very important life lessons can help your children face life with confidence and significance.

A Significant Life
Minimalism can bear fruit and result in the nourishment of several aspects of a better life. Significance is one of them. You can actually track and share your progress of inspiring others to live their lives in a simple way. You can also talk about it with your friends and relatives and help them start their own journeys toward minimalism.

Once you have achieved a minimalist life, your life is becomes your own portfolio that can motivate others who have experienced the same struggle as yours and want to break free. From the amount of money you have collected after selling some of your possessions, why not support a cause or have your own? Remember that money is only as valuable as what we choose to spend it on.

As previously discussed, more is not actually better. Less items of better quality are better. This allows you to enjoy high-quality items in fewer numbers that can be used for years, thus allowing you to save money and time. This is a great scenario that is far better than buying, and buying lots of things that get ruined after several uses.

Once you create a lighter perspective today, everything around you will follow. A less stressful life exuded in the workplace will do wonders; and before you know it, you have already changed someone's life for the better. A less-stressful workplace can lead to a more productive workforce that will exceed expectations.

Happiness in Having Less
This can be tough for individuals who have been living with lots of things around them. These things serve as a massive roadblock that prevents them from seeing the beauty of the

destination that awaits. There is true happiness in having less, because there will be less worries, less stress, and less cost.

Minimalism is Visually Appealing
Because there are fewer things to look at, your guests will appreciate the simple details that deliver an impact. The natural light that passes through glass windows, the gleaming reflection of floor tiles, and much more are simple accents that do make a huge difference.

Of course, when you have less things, finding them will be a piece of cake. It will take you less time to search for items you need because they are already sorted and easier to find.

More Space for the Heart
Once you have successfully burned some bridges, have accepted the things that you cannot change, and have a tighter circle, you allow more space for your heart to give and receive love. Imagine how great that would be.

Among the bridges that need to be burned is your relationship with the past. There is nothing you can do about the past but to accept it and make peace with it so that it will not haunt you in the present and cloud your future. This will promote a lighter heart and will put a smile on your face because you can finally have the peace you've been seeking for years.

Less clutter and fewer things to think about equal less technology. These significant reductions allow the restoration of one of the most important aspects of living a meaningful life – communication. When you have less of the things that clutter your living and emotional space, you promote communication. Switch off the TV and stop tinkering with your mobile phone. Talk, and talk more often face to face.

Breathe

You might forget this. Minimalism allows you to breathe. Breathe often because it calms the soul.

CHAPTER VII – DECLUTTERING FOR THE SENTIMENTAL PERSON

We all know that minimalism might be a problem for the very sentimental person – that individual who cherishes even the tiniest fibers of the scarf given to them by a friend from the other side of the globe or a letter sent by a first love a decade ago. To these individuals, it would be a heart-breaking experience to have the most important items left to be discarded. This even applies to things like toys and other items that have sentimental value that cannot be replaced by any amount of money. These things that are associated with an immense amount of sweet memories are very hard to get rid of.

We all have varying levels of tolerance, and because we can be sentimental at times (or most of the time), this can be a very tough call for some. However, we tend to miss the essence of minimalism. Becoming a minimalist does not mean that there should be none – there should only be less. Here are some less traumatic ways as to how minimalism can work even to the most sentimental person.

Share the Love
If you think that getting rid of your treasured things is too traumatic, why not consider sharing them with friends and relatives? Not only it does lighten the burden, even if you're giving them away, but it also provides a channel through which you can revisit the memories without completely deleting the idea. Love grows, especially when you share.

Repurpose

You can actually repurpose some of your memorable items and combine them, like a wall clock with collage or a framed compilation of small things that is filled with memories. There are numerous repurposing methods you can use depending on what items you are having trouble letting go.

Digitize

Most of the things that add to the bulk are photo albums and framed pictures of your family. With the technology we have nowadays, we have the opportunity to immortalize these images by saving them as digital copies. Digitized images are virtually indestructible, and you can reproduce them as many times as you want to be distributed to friends and loved ones. This also saves a lot of space and time, and you can browse through them when you want, especially if they are saved on a flash drive or DVD.

Start Writing

It is actually a great idea to start writing about your life from two different perspectives – one for your journey as that romantic and very sentimental person who has been surrounded by lots of memorable experiences and items that are heavily soaked with stories, and another as a person who is about to transform his or her life from a hoarding, sentimental individual to a minimalist yet passionate person. This outlet enables you to better detach yourself from the things that you tend to hold on to. This has been one of the outlets that has been used by busy minimalists who started out as struggling families who had a hard time segregating their possessions. You may even end helping others by allowing them to read your life story, and in the end, you can actually gain a friend or a fan in the process.

CHAPTER VIII – BECOMING THE RATIONAL MINIMALIST

"Minimalism is the intentional promotion of the things we most value and the removal of everything that distracts us from it."

—*Joshua Becker*

The problem with most individuals is the way they react and get sweaty whenever they hear the word "minimalism." To the uninformed, minimalism means barren walls and isolation. Right there and then, they come up with the decision to say, "nope, that is not for me." This is one of the major reasons why minimalism remains a lifestyle that not everyone is open to. This is where rational minimalism enters the scene. It is something that is more acceptable because it is not a "hardcore" type. Rational minimalism still hangs on to the discipline of minimalism without being too drastic. If you were to enter the house of a rational minimalist, you would not absorb the idea immediately that a minimalist lives in that place.

A rational minimalist still collects things and lives a normal life with his or her family. These individuals still have some clutter, some possessions that you will not normally find in a minimalist home. So, what makes them minimalist if they still have these things?

It starts with a mindset. Always remember that no one is born as a minimalist. We all have our varying levels of sentimentalism, and we all have the tendency to hold on to things that have stories and memories associated with them. Minimalism starts in us when we appreciate more of what is less. When we appreciate our fewer possessions, we tend to cherish the intangible possessions more. These intangible possessions include love, health, and hope.

Minimalism is holistic, and it does not end with the few things that you have right now. It is a way of life that is sometimes not obvious like a particular diet plan or fashion statement, but it slowly radiates from the inside out. Minimalism is about finding the true meaning of life, where there is happiness and sadness. These sweet notes and bitter memories add flavor to what the true essence of living is all about. In a nutshell, minimalism is like a pair of tweezers that detaches you from the materialistic world in which we live today.

There are also individuals who are labeled as "bandwagoners" because they think minimalism is "in." Unfortunately, this is not a seasonal mindset in which you prefer to live a minimalist life for some time and just revert back to your old ways when you don't feel like doing it anymore.

Doing so will lead to terrible and painful whiplash, especially when you have discarded some of the things that you have no serious intentions of disposing. It is a life-altering decision, because it will surely change your life for the better.

CHAPTER IX – 29 DAYS TO DECLUTTERING YOUR LIFE

You've been well informed at this point regarding what to expect and how to proceed in decluttering your life. According to minimalist experts, one month is the healthiest amount of time to allow individuals to immerse themselves in the process. 29 days, or four weeks of reflection, transformation, reduction, and freedom. The values are negotiable depending on one's emotional and mental strength, but try to stay on track as much as possible. Like any kind of endeavor or project, the first step is the hardest and most critical. This is where most individuals fail, not because they can't do it, but because they are scared to take the first step. You know what to do first?

Breathe...

Physical De-Cluttering
Expected Duration: 7 to 14 Days
Difficulty Level: Moderate to Hard

Now how are we going to start? It is actually simple, and you need to keep it as simple as possible. You can start with baby steps by allotting 10 minutes of each day to sorting a particular space in your home. Other minimalist experts prefer to fix their office spaces first because it is easier to navigate, but it will completely depend on your preference. The 10 minutes will be used to segregate the things found in your preferred spot.

Note: The allotted time can be increased up to thirty minutes maximum. Experts believe that going beyond the half an hour limit can be emotionally dragging on the initiation of this endeavor. The decluttering process should not be overburdening or painful.

Gather things into a pile and segregate them based on these questions:

Do I need it?
Will I still use it?
Do I love it?

If your answer to any of these questions is a "no," then it is time for that particular item to be donated, recycled, or forwarded to someone like a friend or a relative who might want or need it. Place the items in a box for a particular purpose. Once you have successfully completed the first day, congratulate yourself because not everyone has enough courage to do the task that you have just accomplished. Once you've gotten your groove on and got the ball rolling, here are some of the things that you can do on within the next couple of days until the second or third week.

Continue De-cluttering in Small Pieces
You should be able to find a specific area in your home where you can perform your de-cluttering scheme. By focusing on smaller pieces and smaller spaces, you accomplish more each day. Refrain from "shotgun de-cluttering" where you designate several small pieces each day. This will only yield an unproductive de-cluttering session for you.

Simmer Down Your Inner Perfectionist
De-cluttering does not require complex mechanics to make it work. Simple de-cluttering always works, and you can de-

clutter more at a later time when you are more ready.

Get Connected

After several days, you can connect with your friends or relatives to ask if they want or need things that are available in your boxes. This will make the de-cluttering and unloading process a lot easier. There is almost always a friend you have who will be more than willing to receive things from you.

There is a Magic Box

De-cluttering can be tough, but you do not have to crumble and start over. If there are items that are giving you a hard time, you can place them in a "Maybe Box." This box is designed for items that are giving you headaches about whether you will give them away or keep them. Your Maybe Box should have a date, and the maximum allowed time for an item to stay inside is six months. If the item is still there by then, you probably do not need it at all. However, do not overuse this box because it might end up as the first box to get filled up.

Call for Reinforcement

What's a party when no one is with you, right? In general, a de-cluttering project should involve someone who is willing to help you sort things out. Get help from friends or family members, because they can give you sound advice on what to dispose or what to keep or donate. They can even find things they want, which can positively affect your decision to let go of things knowing that they will be going to someone you know.

You'll take pride in how much de-cluttering you've done in just a couple of weeks. We have already accomplished the physical aspect of de-cluttering. We now proceed to the deeper facets of this project.

Professional Life De-Cluttering
Expected Duration: 3 to 7 Days

Difficulty Level: Moderate

De-cluttering your professional life can be one of the easiest or the hardest hurdle depending on what type of an individual you are in the workplace. If you are one of those introverts who treasure e-mails from your co-workers, then this might be a problem for you. To those "life of the party" employees, this might come a bit easier.

Fix Your Inbox

This is applicable to both your personal and company e-mails. It is highly likely that you have a very cluttered mailbox. Clean it by segregating the e-mails that deserve a space in your inbox and deleting those that do not. Remove anything about company gossips and hot issues, and keep in mind that you need to keep your inbox simple and clean. By de-cluttering your inbox, you subconsciously unload some of the professional burdens you have experienced in life because you have been constantly reminded of the stress from the previous e-mails that you've read many times already.

We're not done yet. Clear your phone's inbox as well. Unless there are important details such as phone numbers or addresses, clear them. This will not only free some space in your inbox, but it also inhibits you from looking back at bad moments, including those frustrating ones. It is alright to keep some quotes, if there are any. It is also the best time to delete some of the contacts in both your phone and e-mail address list. Cancel out the potential stressors that can trigger a bad experience, which can lead to distraction and unnecessary stress that could have been prevented in the first place.

I'm sure your inbox is also blooming with newsletters and other online subscriptions. Now is the best time to ask if they benefit you at all. The latest fashions, sports news, best hair care products – do they matter to you at all? What newsletter subscriptions are you willing to de-clutter? Unsubscribe from those mailing lists now.

Revisit Your Calendar

I have yet to see a calendar that is very neat in appearance. Most of the calendars in the office are heavily written with dates, phone numbers, meetings, birthdays, everything. While this is the actual purpose of having an office calendar, it can be a stressful sight to look at. There are several things that can be done with your calendar. First, you can either save a digital calendar or organizer in your computer and then type the scheduled appointments or other professional engagements under the corresponding dates. Next, double-check the appointments that can be cancelled, reduced, or modified. This allows more time for other things, such as single tasking, more prompt time-outs, among others. This also promotes a more simplified schedule, something that is more bearable even by just looking at it.

De-cluttering your schedule is about reducing your engagements and commitments. This is also the part where you should say "no" to some of the avoidable meetings or activities. Revisit your list, prioritize your tasks, and then start de-cluttering your schedule. Whenever necessary, cut down on activities by politely declining invitations that can be avoided and detach yourself from existing commitments.

Physiological De-Cluttering
Expected Duration: 7 to 14 Days
Difficulty Level: Easy to Moderate

Physiological de-cluttering involves the food you eat. This can be tough, but you can always start slowly. Like the milder diet choices that do not include drastic lifestyle modifications, you can cut down on a specific artificial ingredients one at a time. You can also reduce your fast food intake in a tolerable manner. If you've been on a fast food diet for about four to five times a week, try to reduce it to just twice or thrice a week. Once you can sustain this for a week, reduce it further into once or twice a week. Try this reduction technique on subsequent weeks until you can settle for a thrice a month fast food intake.

Hearty Homemade
The good thing about preparing your own meals is that you know where they came from and you know that they are fresh. It saves you a lot of money as well in the end. You can prepare a pre-selected rotation of meals depending on your preference, although try your best to have enough servings of those healthy fruits and vegetables at least once a day. Surprisingly, many employees enjoy meals prepared at home. The sad yet avoidable truth about it is that no one has time to prepare one, but the good news is that minimalism allows you to have more time for stuff like this.

The Essence of Water
Water is still the best hydrating solution for our cells. There may be other options available in the market, but you are leaving clutter inside your system – clutter that comes in the form of preservatives, excess sugar, salt, and artificial coloring. Stay hydrated by imbibing water in its purest form. If you cannot help but to take several cups of coffee each day, try to augment your intake with several glasses of water in between. Excessive caffeine in the bloodstream can cause agitation and palpitations, adverse reactions that water will never give you.

Relax to the Max
I'm not saying that you should just quit your job and go crazy over a relaxing experience. In de-cluttering your system, try to consider relaxation options, such as meditation, massages, and yoga. These activities allow your body to release tension, which is something that rest cannot do on its own. Massages relieve aching muscles, whereas meditation and yoga clarify and calm your mind. These options can help you become more focused and mentally as well as physically prepared for the next workday.

Emotional De-Cluttering

Expected Duration: 7 to 14 Days
Difficulty Level: Moderate to Hard

Emotional de-cluttering is placed last for a reason. Of the four aspects of de-cluttering, this one is permanent. This is about your relationships with your family, relatives, friends, and neighbors. When you have people in your life, de-cluttering can be a complicated process. If you are single, then it can be a good start. Small families can experience quite a challenge, whereas extended families living under the same roof can consider this as one of the biggest hurdles of living a simple yet meaningful life.

Discuss Life Goals
This is something that should not be done in a single discussion. We all have our own virtues, even if we live under the same roof or are from the same family. Each one is unique, and we should not antagonize others because of our differences. Our differences should be used as instruments to complement one another. In discussing life goals, it is very important to hear one another's sides and explain the reasons for engaging in this kind of transformation. This way, all conflicts will be resolved right before the major life changes. Compromise if needed, especially with the younger ones, but teach them about the importance of this activity. We all know that some individuals focus on the benefits but don't like the dirty work. We should be able to lead by example for the other members of the family, especially the children. Allow them to observe how to de-clutter a particular space, and show them how nicer it is after, and how it becomes a lot easier to clean and find things.

Resistance is Normal
Resistance can be present in both homes and workplaces. If this occurs, focus on your space. Do not allow frustration to enter; you'll end up starting over again because you will be overburdened by emotional distress. You should be able to understand since you have been going through life in a cluttered way. Try your very best to empathize, and be

receptive to comments that you hear.

Be Inspired

In times when you feel that nothing is working at all, remember the moment when you started living a simple life. This makes it easier to smile again and move forward. Decluttering is not an easy journey, and it never will be. Like a rocky mountain trail, there will be obstacles that will block your way, and how you respond to it will determine the fate of your journey.

FINAL THOUGHTS..

A minimalistic path can seem like an overwhelming approach to life despite its core values of being simple. Sometimes, we are just too afraid to try things because this approach will require us to let go of things that we are holding on to. Imagine a world of living a simple life, away from distractions and closer to appreciating what the beauty of living is all about – that is what minimalism wants us to experience.

We have discussed the hurdles that you need to defeat and the struggles that you need to free yourself from. We identified the possible options to make this a worthwhile journey rather than a traumatic experience. As minimalist experts have explained, it is something that is worth a try because it will change your perspective on life. In a world in which we are heavily surrounded and smothered by flashing lights and the glaring appeal of today's technology, minimalism is a breath of fresh air and a deeper look at what life is all about.

Whenever life starts to overwhelm you, all you need to do is remember 3 things:

De-clutter..
De-own...
Breathe...

12778641R00032

Printed in Poland
by Amazon Fulfillment
Poland Sp. z o.o., Wrocław